God made every tree in the forest!

"Stop and notice God's miracles."
Job 37:14

**God made the animals that live in the forest.
Can you find five animals hiding in this picture?**

God made this giant redwood tree hundreds of years ago.

God made all these wild flowers.
"Look at the wild flowers. See how they grow."
Luke 12:27

At this western ranch, we can ride horses.

Some horses like to run!

There are lots of interesting sights to see in South Dakota!

God made Mount Rushmore,
and people carved the faces of
four U.S. presidents there.
Do you know which presidents they are?
Unscramble the words below to find out their names.

TONSHAWING _ _ _ _ _ _ _ _ _ _

LOLNINC _ _ _ _ _ _ _

JESFRONEF _ _ _ _ _ _ _ _ _

SEVERLOOT _ _ _ _ _ _ _ _ _

Answers: Washington, Lincoln, Jefferson, Roosevelt (Theodore)

We're taking a balloon ride. God made the air, the sky, and all the earth we see from way up high.

When we're in trouble, God sends help.
"I will not be afraid because the Lord is with me."

Psalm 118:6

God made the Mississippi River, the longest river in the United States.

MISSISSIPPI QUEEN

River too high! Go back 2 spaces.

Take the shortcut bridge, skip 4 spaces.

River blocked, go back 3 spaces.

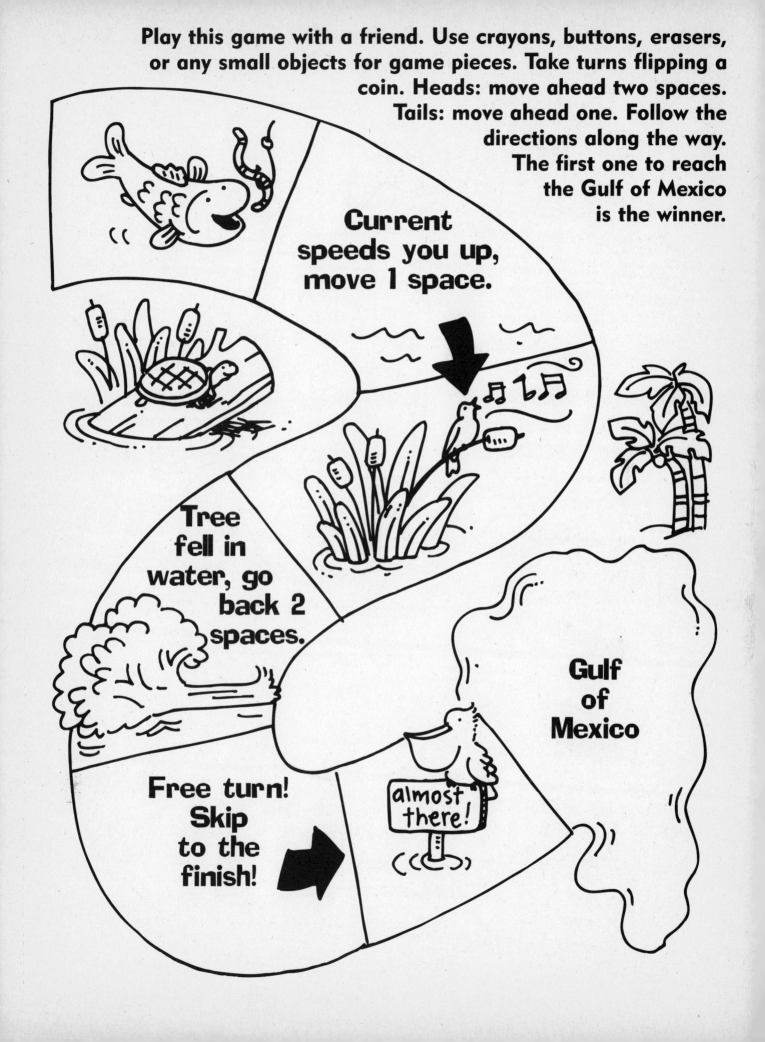

Play this game with a friend. Use crayons, buttons, erasers, or any small objects for game pieces. Take turns flipping a coin. Heads: move ahead two spaces. Tails: move ahead one. Follow the directions along the way. The first one to reach the Gulf of Mexico is the winner.

Current speeds you up, move 1 space.

Tree fell in water, go back 2 spaces.

Free turn! Skip to the finish!

almost there!

Gulf of Mexico

Let's take a riverboat ride!

God made five Great Lakes that look like oceans. Their names are Huron, Ontario, Michigan, Erie, and Superior. They are on the border of the United States and Canada.

God is with us in big cities and little towns.

Chicago is a big city in Illinois.
One of the tallest buildings in the world, the Sears Tower, is there.

Can you find the names of 12 big cities hiding in the puzzle?

CHICAGO   CINCINNATI   DALLAS
DETROIT   LOS ANGELES   MONTREAL
NEW YORK   NEW ORLEANS   PHILADELPHIA
TORONTO   SEATTLE   CALGARY

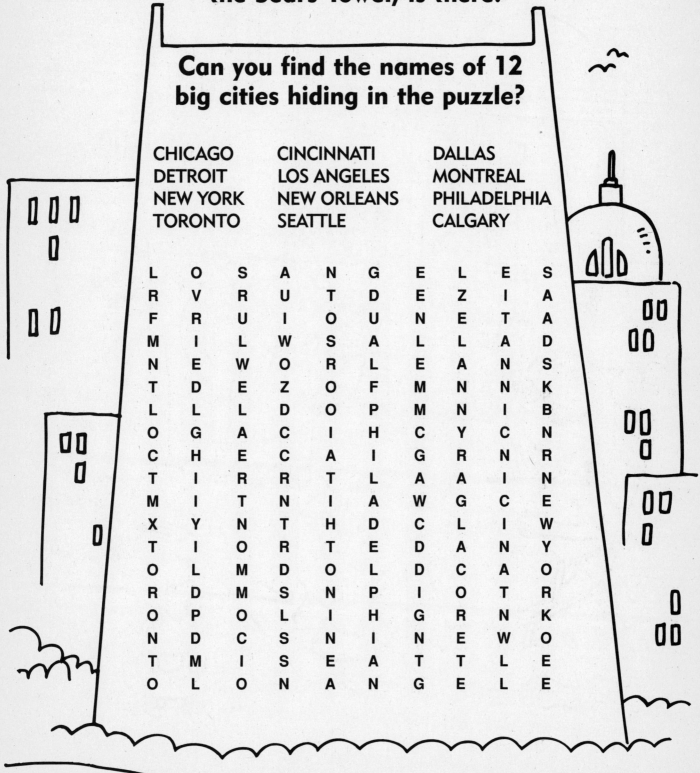

Some places are just for fun!

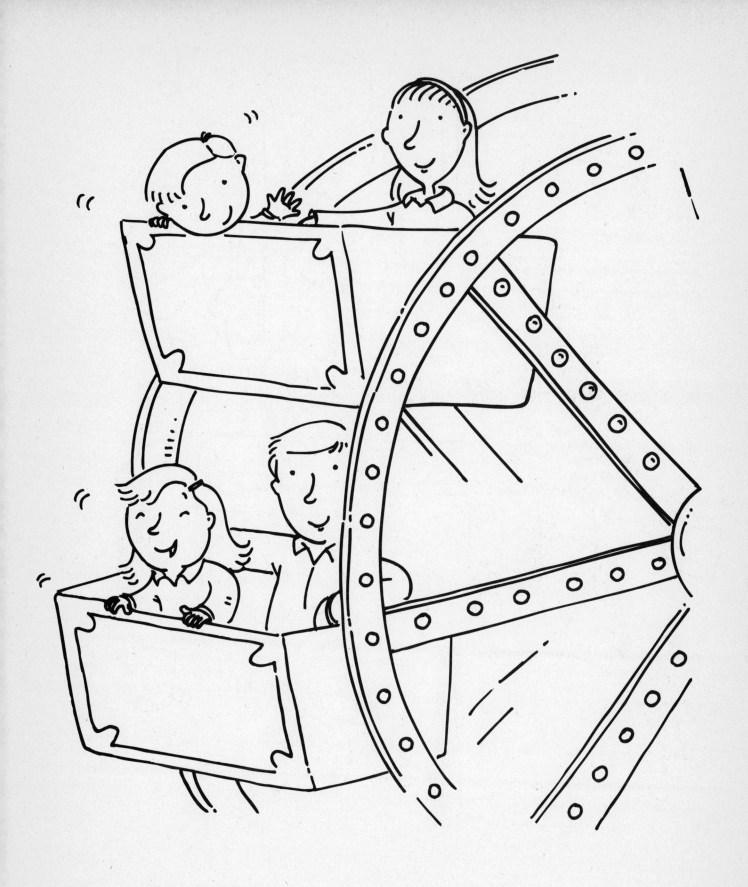

It's great to have fun times with family!

There are ten things that don't belong in this picture. Can you find them?

Remember to pray before you eat.
"Always give thanks to God the Father for everything."
Ephesians 5:20

**This area is a safe place made just for wild birds!
It's called a sanctuary.**

**God's church is called a sanctuary, too.
Let's praise God in his sanctuary!**

from Psalm 150:1

We're going to visit somebody special while we're on vacation. Who is it?
Work the code to find out. Under each letter, write the letter that would come after that letter in the alphabet.
Hint: Z=A.

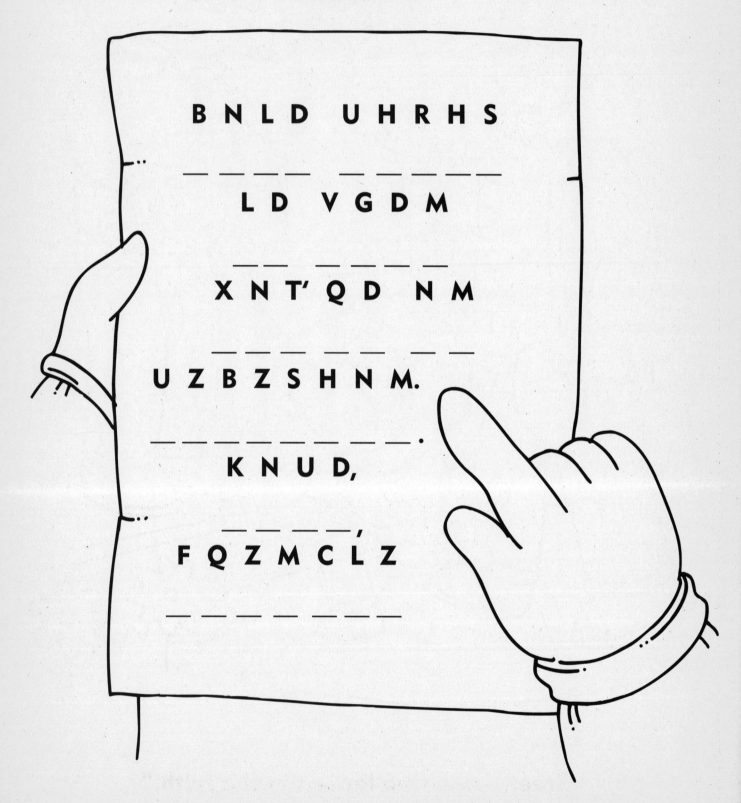

B N L D   U H R H S

_ _ _ _   _ _ _ _ _

L D   V G D M

_ _   _ _ _ _

X N T ' Q D   N M

_ _ _ _ _   _ _

U Z B Z S H N M .

_ _ _ _ _ _ _ _ .

K N U D ,

_ _ _ _ ,

F Q Z M C L Z

_ _ _ _ _ _ _

"Greet those who love us in the faith."

Titus 3:15

Thank you God, for our grandma.

"We should love each other, because love comes from God."
1 John 4:7

Before we leave the zoo, let's play a game. Find at least ten things on these two pages that begin with "p."

**When God made the earth he said,
"Let the earth be filled with animals."**

Genesis 1:24

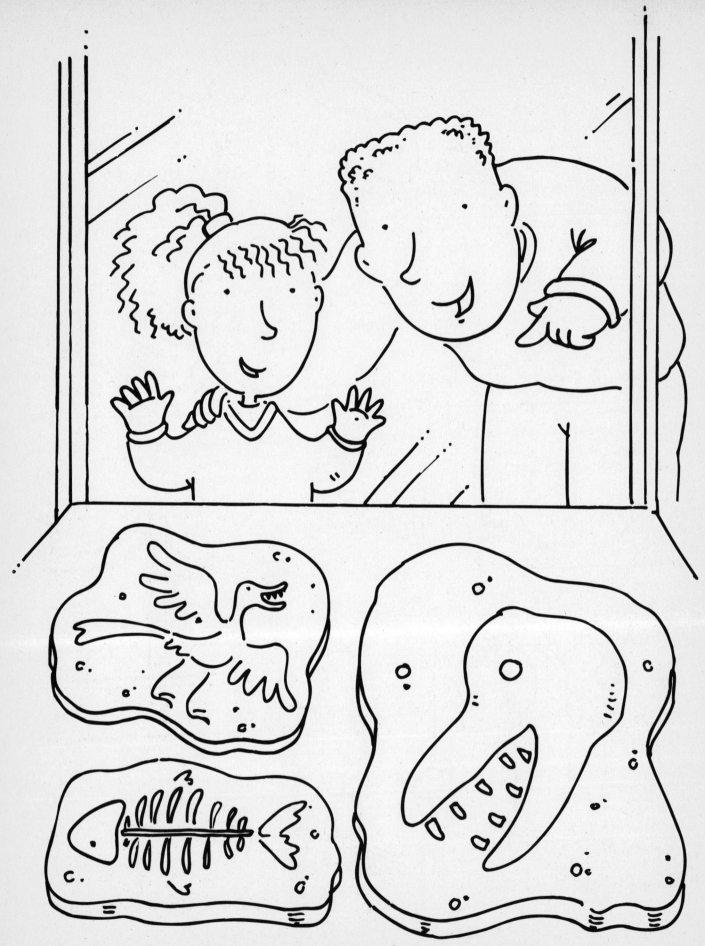

We're at a dinosaur museum!

These fossils tell us how dinosaurs lived long ago.

"Come and see what God has done."
Psalm 66:5

God made so many beautiful places!

no dots = green
1 dot = blue
2 dots = red
3 dots = yellow

The Liberty Bell in Philadelphia is a symbol of freedom for America. Who gives us freedom? To find out, color the spaces according to the key.

Hold this page up to a mirror to see what God says about America.

We're almost there! Where? Follow the road to find out.

**The President of the United States
lives in the White House.
He leads our country, but God rules the earth.
"God is ruler over all rulers and powers."**

Colossians 2:10

The leaders of the United States government work in the Capitol building. Their job is to protect our freedom.

Work the code to see what the Bible says about freedom. Cross out all the Qs. Then read the words that are left.

QQWQQQEQHQQAVQQEF

RQQEEQDQQQOQMBEQCQ

AUQQSECHQRQIQQSQT

MAQDEQQQUQSFQRQQQEE.

The Air and Space Museum in Washington, D.C., has lots of old airplanes. The first airplanes were invented by men who hoped to fly like birds.

Those who trust the Lord will fly like eagles.
from Isaiah 40:31

Let's praise God for our vacation time!

Where did we go on vacation? Find all the places hidden in the puzzle. The word list will help you.

FOREST   MOUNT RUSHMORE
MUSEUM   NIAGARA FALLS
RANCH   SANCTUARY
WHITE HOUSE   ZOO

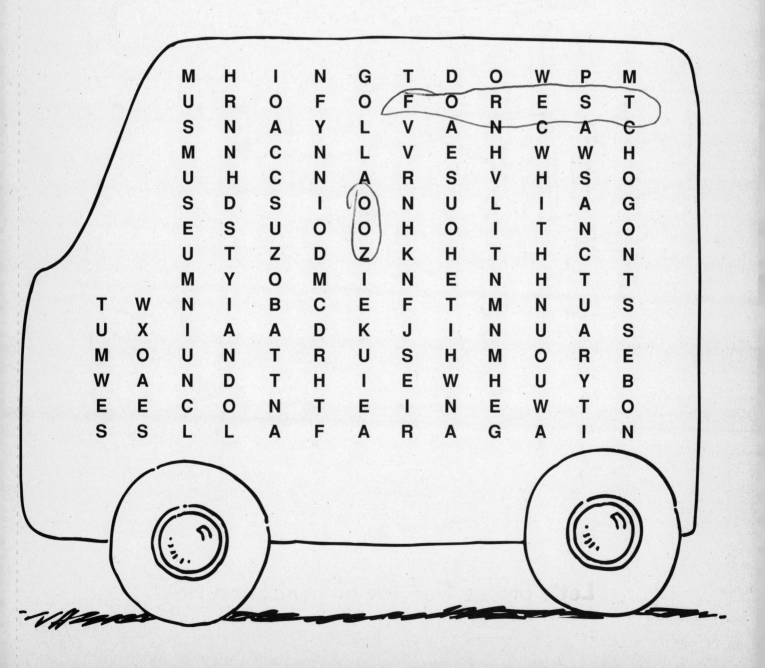

```
M H I N G T D O W P M
U R O F O F O R E S T
S N A Y L V A N C A C
M N C N L V E H W W H
U H C N A R S V H S O
S D S I O N U L I A G
E S U O Z H O I T N O
U T Z D Z K H T H C N
M Y O M I N E N H U T
T W N I B C E F T M N U A S
U X I A D K J I N U A R S
M O U N T R U S H M O R Y E B
W A N D T H I E W H U E B O
E E C O N T E I N E W T O N
S S L L A F A R A G A I N
```

Help this family find the way home. Follow the roads. Which road will take them to their house in California?

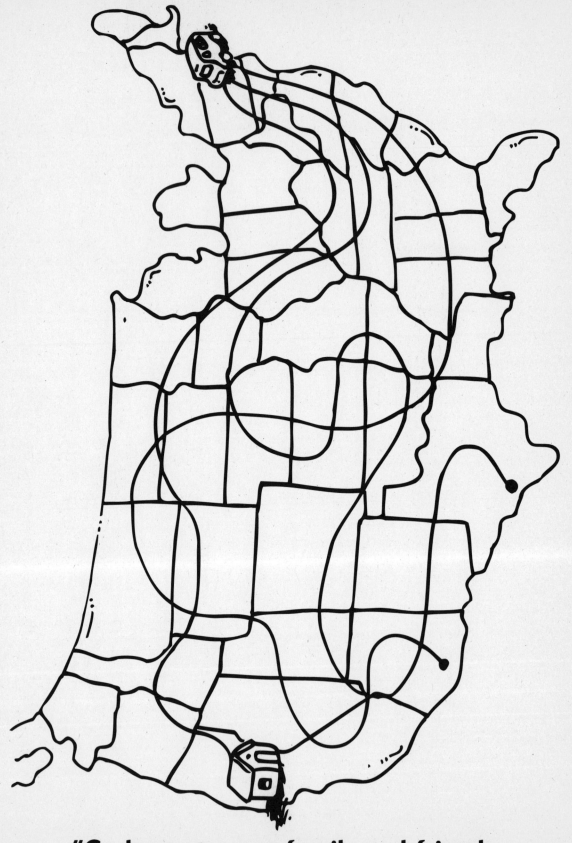

"Go home to your family and friends.
Tell them how much the Lord has done for you."
Mark 5:19